The Inventor's Guide to Success

Mike Kobzan

Published by Mike Kobzan, 2024.

THE INVENTOR'S GUIDE TO SUCCESS

First edition. September 3, 2024.

ISBN: 979-8227080080

Written by Mike Kobzan.

Table of Contents

The Inventor's Guide to Success

By Michael Kobzan

Preface

Inventions can be worth millions. But only if they are protected by a patent. The problem is, this is expensive and without guarantee of returns on the expenditure. Where companies have no problems with high costs, the small independent inventor struggles. He has to see where he can make these costs manageable. This book is all about that. It avoids longwinded explanations where possible and goes step by step through the vagaries of solving this dilemma, how to minimise risks and maximise the chances of success. It explains in simple terms the commonest pitfalls and misconceptions, how to assess risks and recognise chances, how to draw up a strong document of specification for patent registration and finally how to negotiate a contract with prospective industry partners.

Introduction

Intellectual property laws work fine for most creative professions. Artists for instance enjoy strong copyright protection on their works without having to pay a penny. And although technology companies do have to contend with high costs for patent registrations, they usually have comfortable financial reserves to cover these. However, there is a group which finds these laws stacked rather steeply against it, independent innovators working with limited resources. These are all too often intimidated by the high costs of patents not knowing if they will ever see a return on their investment.

But failing to protect one's intellectual property only leads to other intractable problems. Potentially interested industry partners such as manufacturers tend to take a "wheat from the chaff" approach about independent inventions. They only consider them worthy of their attention if "ennobled" with a patent. Even worse, some innovations are so intrinsically simple that anyone will understand them at a single glance. This represents a great risk of the idea slipping into the public domain and thus ruin any chances of filing for a patent at a later date. This leaves many inventors stuck between the wish to capitalise on their ideas, huge financial risk and possibly ruining any chances of exploiting their innovations.

The author, himself an independent inventor with thirty years' experience, goes step by step through the vagaries of how to solve this dilemma and to minimise risks and maximise the chances of success. He explains the commonest pitfalls and misconceptions, how to assess risks and recognise chances, how to draw up a strong document of specification for patent registration and finally how to negotiate a contract with prospective industry partners

The True Chances of Success

L ooking to capitalise on an innovation is a long, arduous and often frustrating process without knowing if all the effort and expense will eventually pay off. So, it is only natural to want to know what the odds are of succeeding before investing time, limited resources and nerves. But ask any patent lawyer and his answer will sound bleak. Of all patents filed globally for registration in any one given year 97% never end up being financially exploited. Put the other way, only 3% are ever financially exploited! And of these it can only be guessed how many successfully return a tangible profit.

Pondering the 3,168,900 patents registered worldwide in 2017, this gives rise to the question, why so many registrations if the success rate is so low?

The main reason lies in the fact that most patents are filed with no intention of ever capitalising on them. This sounds like madness, but there is method to it. Technology companies, the most prolific patent applicants with about 90% of all patents, register most of them speculatively for the sole purpose of securing claims on possible future usage of new technologies. Typically, this happens after a technological breakthrough or when the development of certain technologies looks promising. For example, after the discovery of graphene was announced, companies started filing thousands of patents on prospective new products which exploit this new material. With these they hoped to secure an edge over their competitors or to block possible competing product developments. This also happened when touch screen technology, in its infancy in the 1990s, started to show possible market potential. Another case in point is the graphic user interface, which was still just a research project at Xerox in the early 1980s.

Sudden corporate filings of thousands if not tens of thousands of speculative patents are not even a new phenomenon. Goodyear's discovery, the vulcanisation of rubber 180 years ago, also triggered a whole spate of speculative patents that used this new material. Most of them ended up unused in filing cabinets never to see the light of day again. This practice has resulted in companies sitting on portfolios of tens of thousands of patents with no intention of ever using them other than as leverage in business negotiations, in intellectual property court cases or as an asset in the evaluation of a company.

Another category that makes up a large part of that 97% is what might be called hindrance patents. These are filed when a company develops a complex product that is technically already long in the public domain, such as an internal combustion engine, and wants to hinder the design being copied too easily. For this a number of patents are filed on certain aspects of the product. These could be the bolt positions of the exhaust manifold, the design of the housing, the position of the valves, the shape of the oil sump or the position of the oil filter etc. Because these are specifically designed and arranged in a certain way unique to the product they could be claimed, if argued the right way, to fulfil the perquisites of patent law. One can argue that these patents are exploitable; after all they protect a product that contributes to the success of the company. But the technology they are protecting is not the engine even if that is the end result. They are protecting the design and arrangement of a few components unique to that particular product. In any other context outside of the parent product they do not have any value to anyone.

What this all tells us is that of the 97% unexploited patents, 70%, at a conservative guess, are dormant and lay unused in some database or filing cabinet or are valueless outside of their parent product. Take these patents out of the calculation and suddenly the success rate of patents intended for financial exploitation rises to at least 10%.

Improving the Odds

One might now think that a 10% probability of success is still a pretty daunting gamble to a lone innovator who plans to invest a good part of their life savings in their brainchild. It is important though to note that this has nothing to do with gambling. Those 10% are not successful because of some stroke of good luck, they are successful because the innovations prove to have a high market potential. The other 90% fail because they are missing this. In other words, one has to first gauge an innovation's market potential to see if it is among those 10% before further investing time and money.

For many innovators this is usually a difficult step to take because it forces them to face reality and often give up on a much-cherished idea. So, here, to begin with a few words to help make things easier:

It is only natural to be enthusiastic about a novel idea born of sudden inspiration. It is what gives people the drive to build successful businesses, write great books, become film stars and rock idols or launch political careers. But enthusiasm alone can never be a substitute for potential. Success is built on both, if potential is missing success will remain elusive.

The same can also be said of inventors and their ideas. There is a great danger of blindly investing time and money in an untested idea in the erroneous belief that enough effort will compensate for any possible shortcomings. This is not to say perseverance, determination and dogged belief in one's idea is wrong. When the going gets tough it is often the crucial element for success. But such steadfastness has to be objectively justified and not just based on some vague "good feeling". This means keeping rational no matter how promising one's idea might first appear, to keep an emotional distance and honestly ask oneself if it really is something people will willingly pay good money for. If there is any doubt in the answer, it is probably better to have the wisdom to leave it be.

Gauging Market Potential

Admittedly, this is not an exact science. There can never be an absolutely reliable answer to the market potential of an innovation; there are simply too many parameters, unpredictable variables and unknowns. But these can be narrowed down somewhat by taking a good, hard, critical look at the weaknesses and strengths of one's innovation. Big companies do this all the time with new products and services. They even employ whole marketing departments for it, but this does not necessarily mean that one single person cannot do the job just as well.

A prime example is the late Steve Jobs whose legendry talent for spotting good, marketable ideas singlehandedly turned a failing computer manufacturing business into one of the most valuable consumer technology enterprises in the world.

There are two requirements for gauging the marketability of an innovation. The first is to have a certain familiarity with the targeted consumer group. These are the prospective users one assumes will most likely benefit from the product and buy into it. This of course has to be assumed of anyone claiming to have an innovative solution to a problem and therefore requires no further explanation.

The second is a list of criteria to evaluate the strengths and weaknesses of an innovation. These are slightly more challenging to define since each and every innovation has its own characteristics and addresses its target group in its own particular way. Criteria paramount to the market potential of one invention might be negligible to another. The following criteria are therefore generic, they do not claim in their entirety to be all-inclusive in a way that delivers absolute clarity and are meant more to sensitise the reader to think of further criteria specific to their innovation.

Criteria That Reduce Market Potential

<hr>

1) **The invention is an alternative to an already existing solution.**

An example of this is the power transmission of a bicycle. The conventional technologies in use today are of course the chain drive and belt drive introduced in the late 1800s. These have proven sufficient over the years and offer near to 100% mechanical efficiency. This has not deterred inventors from developing superior solutions which usually involve combinations of cranks, levers, connecting rods, pulleys, cables, cogs and shafts.

These concepts generally do offer benefits of kinds over conventional solutions, but they also create other problems. For instance, they are usually not compatible to stock components such as frames, brakes, luggage racks, mud guards, pedals and gear systems. They are also usually far more complex than the solutions they are supposed to replace. Manufacturers will therefore shy away from such innovations as long as the benefits do not clearly outweigh the problems that they cause.

Avoid solutions to problems that have already been solved unless there is a huge and clear benefit to be had.

2) The invention contravenes social norms.

These are ideas that do not necessarily break any laws, but are still unacceptable to most of society. One example is the emergency receptacle for motorists stuck in traffic jams desperate to relieve themselves without being able to leave their vehicles. Although the practical benefits are undeniable, most consumers would be put off by the very thought of its use.

3) The invention requires its own infrastructure.

Cars would be pretty impractical without a network of gas stations. Electrical home appliances would be useless without power lines to deliver electricity. TVs and radios would have no practical use without the TV and radio stations to produce content for them. And without their network of transceivers, mobile phones would be just expensive paperweights. The value of all these modern conveniences hinges on one kind of infrastructure or another.

Behind the introduction of the above products are big market players and state interests that readily secure the frame work of laws and finance for their infrastructures. It is doubtful at best that even the most ambitious independent inventor has the influence and ability to secure such support.

Case in point is a novel bicycle stand that serves also as a lock to secure the bicycle to a unique fixture anchored in the ground. Certainly, a bicycle secured in such a fashion is safe from theft. But an effective utilisation of this idea demands that wherever cyclists need to secure their bicycles, someone has to first introduce these unique ground fixtures. It would take years, maybe even decades, if at all, to convince local authorities, businesses, schools etc. to invest in such infrastructure before this innovation is of any benefit to the user.

4) The invention is a novelty for novelty's sake.

For this we first need to delve slightly into patent law. This stipulates three prerequisites for registering patents:

An invention must, a) have a high level of novelty, b) offer at least one solution to a problem and c) be financially exploitable.

Prerequisite a) is nearly always subject to the highest scrutiny and is the most difficult to fulfil. On the other hand, perquisite b) is with clever wording in the patent specifications relatively easy to fulfil. And as for perquisite c) any claim of financial exploitability cannot be disproven. Who's to say that even the most ridiculous idea will not find at least one buyer?

This has led to the phenomenon of patents for inventions that at face value do not solve any problems; they're novelties for novelty's sake. As a rule, the market potential of such inventions tends towards zero.

But there are exceptions.

One example is the drinking straw invented in 1888 by a certain Mr Marvin Stone. At the time, the idea fulfilled the first prerequisite, it was new. But otherwise, there are simply no plausible advantages to drinking beverages through straws.

The epic success of the drinking straw is rather due to a combination of novelty appeal, party appeal, extremely low manufacturing costs and establishments looking for novel ways to entice patrons onto their premises. If a novelty invention has all that behind it, it is possibly going to be a winner, otherwise it is advisable to just leave it be.

5) The innovation will soon be made obsolete by foreseeable technological progress.

An example of this, albeit strictly speaking not an invention, was the Ford Company's plans in the early 1900s for a huge rubber tree plantation complete with a town and housing for the workers in South America in the early 1900s.

At the time there was serious concern that the growing global demand for rubber would soon exceed the supply and such a plantation would secure the company enough latex to weather any shortages and rising prices. Needless to say, before the plantation could start production the chemical industry announced the invention of cheap synthetic rubber.

6) The innovation needs supporting technology that is not yet advanced enough.

The dream of flying cars is a typical case in point. Inventors have been designing and building prototypes now since the mid-1900s, usually with the proud announcement that they have finally cracked it. Soon the skies will be full of their flying vehicles effortlessly avoiding traffic congestion as they bring their happy owners hassle free to their destinations.

This of course has not been the case, mainly because the technologies of the day compromise the usability of the vehicles too much. This is not to say that such vehicles will never become a reality. Developments in fields such as high efficiency electro-motors, high-capacity accumulators, light-weight materials and, last but not least, autonomous piloting systems are constantly making advances. These will for sure one day make the flying car a ubiquitous mass product. Just not right now.

7) The potential market is dominated by a business syndicate, cartel or monopolist.

It is a bitter experience for any inventor to fail to find acceptance for their innovation even though its benefits and marketability are indisputable. There are many reasons for such failure, but one of the singular most common is that the potential market is dominated by some sort of cartel, syndicate or monopolist.

These are nearly always very protective of their markets, especially against competitive newcomers, and are wary of new, disruptive technologies that could "rock the boat". One can argue that in most industrialised countries such "business arrangements" are illegal, but they do exist, sometimes even with tacit government approval. It is therefore better to avoid innovations that may come against such resistance.

8) The potential market is highly specialised and narrow.

Lucrative innovations profit off large markets with high sales volumes. The narrower and more specialised the market is the lower the sales potential will be. In some cases, the market is so narrow and specialised that even a very good idea does not find enough potential to justify investing in.

As always, there are exceptions to this, for instance when an innovation is so beneficial that it justifies a very high price. One example is the invention of the high precision gyro-theodolites GYROMAT by the German company, Deutsche Montan Technologie GmbH. This device ensured that French and UK engineers building the Channel Tunnel perfectly met in the middle under the English Channel. Today, building long tunnels under large bodies of water or mountains is unthinkable without this invention.

Criteria That Enhance Market Potential

---

1) The invention reduces costs.

Nothing enhances market potential more than the promise of saving money and that's why the majority of successful inventions fulfil this criterion.

Such inventions accomplish this in many different ways. One example is the development of plastics that inhibit electrostatic charge. Before these, all fuel tanks and canisters had to, by law, be made of metal. The reason; normal plastics in contact with liquid fuels have the worrying property of building up a static electrical charge. This represents a serious fire hazard. Since this invention, fuel tanks and canisters can be manufactured far cheaper out of plastics with the added advantage of reduced weight.

Savings can also be indirectly achieved. An invention that greatly increases the service intervals of machinery will reduce service costs. One example is the invention of the hydrostatic valve for internal combustion engines, which greatly reduced the need to regularly set valve clearances.

Reducing the number of parts of given products without compromising performance will usually reduce manufacturing costs. An innovation that simplifies a task, which is otherwise the domain of skilled and therefore high-cost personnel, reduces expenses.

There is a caveat though to cost saving inventions. The benefits have to clearly outweigh the costs of the implementation of the new technology. For manufacturers, amortization within the first three years is considered acceptable. Private users might have different formulae, but cost benefits will still have to be clearly discernible to be attractive.

2) The invention enhances a given product's utility or performance.

One of Steven Wozniak's most ingenious ideas was a simple way of depicting colour on a computer monitor using just a few lines of software code and a one-dollar chip.

Another invention in this category that arguably changed the course of history was James Watt's steam condenser. Adding this to the Newcomen atmospheric engine, at the time a simple reciprocating device in widespread use for pumping water out of mines, increased the power and efficiency enormously. This in turn opened up the possibility of attaching a flywheel and turning the machine into a true rotational one. From there the rest is history with Watt's machine helping to kick-start the industrial revolution.

3) The invention simplifies the operation of an otherwise challenging product.

A good example here is the invention of the photographic film cartridge in 1884 by a certain Mr George Eastman of Kodak fame. This did away with unwieldy and delicate photographic glass plates and opened up photography to the masses.

A more recent example is Xerox's PARC, the very first computer graphic user interface developed in 1979 and today ubiquitous in the field of computer technology. Before then computers offered only a so-called command line interface for user input and machine output, which demanded memorizing hundreds of often intimidatingly abstract commands. This severely limited computer access to only specially qualified personnel, who took months or even years to train.

After Apple adapted the Xerox PARC for their Lisa and later Macintosh PCs, working on computers became a much more intuitive experience allowing users to begin producing meaningful results within just a few hours of training. One could arguably claim that without this innovation the internet and smartphones as we know them today would be unthinkable.

4) The invention helps to alleviate an ecological problem without interfering with the user's habits.

In the mid-1980s the world discovered that CFCs were the prime cause for the rapid decrease of the ozone layer. Because of this, everyone expected the abrupt end of the much-loved aerosol canister, which at the time commonly used CFC gases as a propellant. This did not happen of course because it then practically "rained" inventions for CFC free aerosols as innovators all over the world rushed to file patents.

Ecological innovations are probably the only category in which people are prepared to pay a premium for a good conscience if it spares them the discomfort of having to change their habits. It is one of the prime forces behind the rise of electrically powered vehicles, energy saving light bulbs, intelligent central heating thermostats, wind generators, solar collectors, the sleep and energy saving modus of most electronic devices, low energy refrigerators and of course the CFC-free aerosol; all innovations that let us keep our habits without a bad conscience.

Here we come to the end of the list, but this does not exhaust all possibilities. The above represents only a small choice of the many possible criteria that can influence the market potential of a given invention and is meant as an incentive to think of further criteria.

The Patent Survey

Once adequate market potential has been determined the next step is to question the novelty of the innovation. Is there no prior art, no former invention or technology that is, that could be used to challenge it? Although most inventors will swear blind to this, the question should not be taken lightly. The history of intellectual property litigation is full of cases of already granted patents later being declared invalid. Mostly because plaintiffs have found what is called "prior art" in patent lawyer circles. These are earlier innovations that invalidate a claim of novelty, usually by way of a prior patent that describes the same or similar innovation.

This is bad enough when the prior patent in question expired long ago, but can become a nightmare when it is still valid. Then accusations of intellectual property theft and demands for compensation can follow. It is therefore a good idea to test the novelty of an idea regardless of how convinced one is of it before investing further time and money.

One way to do this is to employ the services of patent surveyors who search through repositories of patent specification documents for prior art. It is worth noting here though that the fees for such services are gauged to a more commercial clientele who have the means to comfortably afford high expenditures.

So, is there a way of getting around these costs? Yes, there is if one is prepared to take the time and afford the effort. Since patent offices in most countries have now placed their archives on-line free of charge to the public, they are no longer the exclusive domain of professional patent surveyors. There is therefore nothing to stop anyone going on line and using these for their own patent survey. As always though, there are a few caveats to consider before doing this.

a). There is no such thing as a comprehensive patent archive. This is especially true of those kept on-line by national patent offices, which only archive patents filed in that particular country. This though is far less of a problem than it first appears. Globally, most patents are filed in the EU and the US with the EU even running a centralised archive of all EU national patent offices together with a few from outside the EU. These two of course make trawling through numerous national archives unnecessary and are consequently the ones a survey should focus on. Never-the-less, it is still important to keep the possibility in mind that a patent specification document is lying unused in an obscure archive somewhere that describes prior art.

b). Patents going back a hundred years or more are sometimes not included in on-line archives. This is particularly frustrating because, regardless of age, the technology explained in expired patents is still considered prior art that effectively voids the novelty claim of any later patent that describes the same idea. Again, in most instances this should not be too big a problem if one is seeking to register a patent for the novel use of later technology, for instance, integrated circuits or high-tech materials etc. or the innovation itself embodies advanced technology.

c). Nearly all national patent offices demand patents be filed in the national language. This most certainly represents a hindrance to anyone not familiar with the national languages of the countries in question. The solution of course is to use an on-line translator which will offer at least a gist of what the original text is about, but with the risk of important points and details getting lost in translation. This risk can be reduced to a certain extent by using different on-line translators on the same text. Because these translators all use their own unique algorithms the results will vary slightly and highlight the discrepancies.

d.) Not only prior art in the form of an earlier patent can be used to void a claim of novelty. Publications in magazines, books, television and on the internet can be just as damaging. To sufficiently survey all this is beyond anyone's capabilities, but this applies also in the other direction. Anyone looking in such publications for prior art against a novelty claim will find the search just as daunting.

As mentioned above, the two globally most comprehensive on-line patent databases are run by the United States Patent and Trademark Office (USPTO) and the European Patent Office (EPO). Patents in the US archive are all in English. The European archive though is actually a combination of all European patent offices and even some from further afield such as China and Japan; so, many of the patents will be in other languages.

United States Patent and Trademark Office:

http://appft.uspto.gov/netahtml/PTO/index.html

European Patent Office:

https://worldwide.espacenet.com/

These websites offer search engines to generate hits and further options to narrow these down to more relevant documents. This can be best exemplified on the following USPTO website:

http://patft.uspto.gov/netahtml/PTO/search-adv.htm

Here it is possible to limit searches to certain parts of patents called "fields" or sections using their "Field Names" such as "Applicant Name", "Inventor Name" etc. In most cases though, only information within the fields "Title", "Abstract", "Claims", "Description/Specification" is of interest. A search within these fields does not necessitate defining these in a search box.

A search begins easily enough by writing a keyword into the query box, for instance "chain" (without the inverted commas) if an innovation is related to such technology. The results can be narrowed down, for instance to only motorcycle technology, by adding "AND motorcycle" (without the inverted commas). This will produce hits that only have the terms "motorcycle" and "chain" within them. If a search word is made up of two words, such as "chain drive", it should be written within inverted commas. This produces results that contain this string of words. For more information on how to refine searches, please visit the following site:

http://patft.uspto.gov/netahtml/PTO/help/helpadv.htm

After hitting the search button, the search engine will show a maximum of fifty of the most recently filed patents together with their titles and their registration numbers. There are probably more waiting to be called up if the search word is not refined enough. The actual amount will be displayed at the top left-hand corner of the screen and can be called up by clicking on the "next 50 hits" button just below.

Note: in the European archive an English keyword will not include patents in other languages, for instance in German or French. That is, the search word has to be entered in the corresponding language to search archives for patents in other languages. Another caveat is the differences in US, British and even former British colony terminology and spelling. For instance, in electrical engineering the term "relay" can also be spelled "relais" and engineers and car mechanics in the British automotive industry often use the term "solenoid" instead of "relay".

By using advanced search methods, it is possible to reduce the results from a few hundred to maybe 20 or 30 hits.

There is another search method suggested by the US Patent and Trademark Office called the "Seven Steps Strategy" explained on their website that might also be useful:

https://www.uspto.gov/learning-and-resources/support-centers/

patent-and-trademark-resource-centers-ptrc/resources/seven

After a search has been refined to more relevant results and the number of hits reduced to a minimum, the survey starts to become more work intensive. That is, the contents of the results have to be read through, document for document. This though is a far less intimidating endeavour than it first appears. Patent specifications always begin with a so-called abstract that summarises the content of the patent document. A click on a search result brings up the corresponding document in a simplified HTML format usually with the abstract in the heading.

Note: this format does not show any images.

The abstract effectively supports a cursory assessment of the content and in most cases should not take more than a few minutes to read through to determine its relevance.

A further way to assess the relevance of a patent lays in the fact that most patent scripts use illustrative depictions to help describe the ideas within them. These often offer at a glance enough insight into the claims of the patent without having to go into the time robbing depths of reading the whole document.

To see these, first click on the "images" button at the top. This will bring up the PDF-formatted first page of the document. A further click on the "full document" button on the left side of the screen will show the whole document with all the illustrations.

Note: There is often no search and find function in these PDF-files.

Ideally, after all these steps, there should not be any patents left in question and the survey is over. But if there are, it is imperative that these are carefully read through. Focus should first be given to the description section of the document where the exact technical workings of the innovation in question are explained point for point. This is followed by the claims section where all the claims made in the description are listed separately. It is advisable to also read this list carefully through because it often includes further claims that are not mentioned in the description section.

Of course, if one's idea is recognisable in one of these documents, this might represent prior art. In such cases it is worth making a closer comparison to see if the claims in the document only come near to one's innovation, that both ideas are maybe not quite the same. It could be just one single detail, maybe a simplification in design, a choice of more advanced materials or modern surface treatment that makes an improvement novel enough to fulfil the prerequisites of patent law. If this is the case, it is a good idea to keep copies of such documents for future reference; they will be needed when it comes to drawing up one's own patent specification document.

The Patent Specification Document

If by now the potential and novelty of an innovation have been assured, the next step is to draw up a patent specification document. This document describes one's innovation and is handed into the patent office to register a patent. It forms the legal basis for protecting one's intellectual property. Depending on the complexity of the innovation, it might be worth commissioning a patent lawyer for this. The patent lawyer has qualifications in at least one field of engineering as well as in law and specialises in intellectual property law. Some countries, for instance Germany, also allow normal lawyers to offer their services in patent law often at very competitive fees to their patent lawyer colleagues. This might be very tempting, but the issue here is that such lawyers, as competent as they surely are in jurisprudence, will hardly have qualifications or experience in any field of engineering. This can pose a problem given that a lawyer is expected to fully grasp the essence of a technical innovation to be able to competently draw up patent specifications.

On the other hand, patent lawyers with their unique qualifications and expertise command some of the highest fees for their services among their lawyer peers. Fifteen thousand to well over thirty thousand USD, depending on complexity, per patent specification and registration is typical. This is why lawyer fees nearly always represent the largest part of an inventor's expenditure.

All this of course is bitter for the lone inventor on a modest budget, but there is a third option, a DIY patent.

Some might balk at this suggestion and it is fair to say that drawing up such a document is not to be taken lightly. In principle it is a contract with the state, which agrees to protect the intellectual property from theft on the basis of the description and claims written in the document. And, as with all good contracts, it has to be "water tight", no loopholes and no ambivalence.

There is a big upside to a DIY patent though. No one single person understands the technology of an innovation better than the actual inventor. Also, patent specifications are hardly works of literary art. Quality of prose does not factor into them at all; emphasis is placed far more on clear, plain English (or the language of choice), with as little specialist terminology, judicial or otherwise, as possible. Any inventor able to express themselves clearly and grammatically correct in written form should have no trouble describing their innovation and as such should be able to draw up a valid patent specification document.

For DIY patents the US patent office (USPTO) offers comprehensive insight into guidelines on everything to do with registering patents on their website under "General information concerning patents".

https://www.uspto.gov/patents-getting-started/general-information-concerning-patents

Here lies a treasure of information describing among other things the different kinds of patent applications, fees, what can be patented etc. There are special sections dedicated to assisting small entities that are especially helpful to the independent inventor.

"Inventors Assistance Center":

https://www.uspto.gov/learning-and-resources/support-centers/inventors-assistance-center-iac

"Inventor and entrepreneur resources":

https://www.uspto.gov/learning-and-resources/inventorsentrepreneurs-resources

The information on this website is of course valid within the US, but not necessarily in its entirety in other countries. It is therefore advisable to be well informed of a country's patent laws before filing for patent registration there.

Guidelines for drawing up patent specification documents are found under the subheading "Specification [Description and Claims]" and should first be read through before beginning:

https://www.uspto.gov/patents-getting-started/general-information-concerning-patents#heading-17

Patent specifications drawn up according to these guidelines are generally accepted by patent offices in most other countries outside the US, albeit usually only in the national language of these countries. The worst that can happen is that a patent office of a different country requests revision of a patent specification according to their guidelines. These are usually just formalities such as cross-referencing conventions, text margins, sheet format etc.

Drawing Up Strong Patent Specifications

Now, as helpful these websites and guidelines are, they fail to explain a number of important aspects of a patent specification document. Among them and probably the most important is, how to make it water tight, that is, how to avoid loopholes and exploitable weaknesses. The following will therefore focus on this subject.

Understanding descriptions and claims

USPTO guidelines require patent specifications be divided into sections with headings such as "Abstract", "Background of the Invention", Brief Summary of the Invention", "Description", "Claims", etc. More about these later. By far the most important of these, in actual fact the essence of the patent specification, are the description and claims sections. In these anything written is legally binding; that is, it contributes to the patent's protective properties. In the description section the innovation and its function are disclosed as clearly and as comprehensively as possible. This is then followed by the claims section. This section reiterates the individual concepts in the description section in the form of a list of claims. A patent specification can have any number of claims, but must have at least one to be accepted by the patent office.

Each claim formulates one single novel idea preferably in one single sentence, but can encompass more if necessary. Under certain circumstances claims to concepts not mentioned in the description can also be made. For instance, if an element is described as a shaft in the description section, a claim can be added stating that this can also have a profile other than cylindrical. But claims cannot suggest parts that are not illustrated or mentioned in the description.

Note: some patent offices' registration fees are calculated according to how many claims are made.

Claims are always assigned the label "claim" followed by a number, i.e., "claim 1, …", "claim 2, …" etc. for cross-reference purposes in other sections of the patent and even in other claims. More on crossreferencing later.

Be prolific with words.

According to the USPTO, descriptions and claims should not only clearly convey the innovation in such a way that a person qualified in the field of the innovation can understand them, they must also be concise. Obviously, they must be clear, but it is misleading to ask for them to be concise.

Concise prose might look elegant and even make for easy reading, but the purpose of a patent specification is not to provide easy reading; it is there to avoid confusion, ambivalence, loopholes and other exploitable weaknesses. It is advisable to be concise where it is safe to do so, but to rather err in direction of being verbose when unsure. It is perfectly correct to fill a page if that is needed to sufficiently explain just one single but maybe complex idea. Nobody in the patent office will reject it; in fact, possibly no one there will ever read it.

Often, when drawing up patent specifications, the validity of a claim is uncertain. There is doubt about its novelty, it seems to be a repeat in principle of another claim elsewhere in the document or it might look unapplicable for other reasons. It is good practice to write in the claim regardless. Invalid claims do not invalidate the rest of the document, the worst that can happen is that the disputed claim is struck from the patent.

Note: While deleting claims from a patent is allowed, the opposite is not possible. Once a specification document has been sent to the patent office for registration it cannot be added to. The rule of thumb therefore is that there can never be too much text or claims in a patent specification. Should an additional claim be necessary, this can only be done by applying for registration of a separate patent specification document.

Avoiding Loopholes and Exploitable Weaknesses

Successful innovative products very often attract people looking for exploitable weaknesses in the patent protection in an attempt to circumvent it. Drawing up a patent specification is therefore comparable to designing a fortress or castle of old that offers protection against possible attack. It is important to anticipate weaknesses and be wary of inadvertently introducing them into the defences. The following dos and don'ts will help avoid this.

Do not use terminology that suggests manufacturing methods.

"Drill holes" for example indicates how these holes are to be manufactured. Anyone could therefore manufacture the holes by other means than drilling and in this way circumvent the patent. Rather refer to any kind of holes as just holes or openings regardless if they are for bolts, ventilation, sensors etc. How these are ultimately fashioned is of no consequence to the patent.

Do not refer to casings, housings, supporting structures etc. as assemblies or fabrications.

Casings, housings and supporting structures etc. are usually assembled or fabricated from machined parts, stock material, castings etc. Unless integral to the innovation, these elements should be treated as single one-piece parts irrespective of how they are ultimately manufactured. If assemblies are integral to the innovation do not specify the method of securing their component parts together, i.e., welded, glued, bolted, brazed etc. If this is unavoidable, emphasize that the method mentioned is just an example and that any suitable fixture technology that fulfils the function of the innovation is applicable. If an assembly joint is semi-permanent, that is to say the parts are meant to be separated again, possibly using a tool, then this should be referred to as semi-permanent without specifying the kind of fixture technology. Avoid mentioning the use of screws, bolts, bayonet locks etc. If for some reason this is unavoidable, it must be emphasised that these are just examples out of many other possibilities.

Caution when specifying materials

If the characteristics of a certain material are important, for instance the elasticity of rubber, the conductivity of copper, the abrasion resistance of ceramic etc., try to specify only the material properties without referencing the material itself. If this results in an unclear description, then describe the material characteristics, make reference to a material and emphasise that this is just an example and that any suitable material that fulfils said properties is applicable. Of course, if the use of a certain material is central to an innovation, i.e., ceramic brake rotors, then the material should by all means be clearly specified.

Caution with stock material.

Depending on the circumstances, dimensions can be open invitations to circumvent the patent and should be used only when absolutely essential. But even if avoided, they can still creep in when stock material is specified such as used in the fabrication of supporting structures or housings, i.e., girders, tubing, sheet metal etc. Stock material is just another term for material manufactured according to national standards specifications. These state standardised dimensions and material characteristics and are no different from how nuts and bolts are standardised. Using the words "stock", "stock material", "Sheet metal" or referring to parts made of stock therefore implies a certain range of dimensions that could be circumvented by using non-stock material. If mentioning stock material is unavoidable then it is a good idea to add the generic term: "...or suitably dimensioned material".

Avoid specialist terminology wherever possible

Terminology exclusive to narrow, specialised fields is not recognised for use in patent specifications and is usually not conducive to patent protection. A whole list of terminology in English and French recognised for use in patent specifications is offered on the WIPO IP Portal:

https://www.wipo.int/classifications/ipc/ipcpub

Otherwise, wherever possible, use terminology that is in broader usage. If the use of a specialised term is unavoidable, for instance without it would make the description overly complex, a definition of the term in plain language should first proceed the use of the specialised term.

Caution about hidden loopholes creeping in.

This is best explained with an example. Assuming an invention comprises a cylinder with a piston inside it. It is specified that the piston is pressed by a spring at one end against the other end of the cylinder where a valve has been installed. One might formulate the claim to this mechanism as follows:

Claim #: "A piston 1 inside a cylinder 2, as illustrated in Fig. 1, is pressed by a spring 3 in such a way that it is held against a valve 4 allocated at one end of the cylinder 1." (The reference numbers, 1,2, 3,4 and Fig 1 will be explained later.)

What at first glance looks like a strong claim has in fact a hidden loophole. The reason: a cylinder by definition has a circular cross-section to its longest axis. Anyone could therefore circumvent the claim by making the cross-section anything other than circular, i.e., elliptical or square.

One solution is to avoid using the term "cylinder" and instead describe it as a volume of space defined by its confines within a casing or housing as illustrated in Fig. 1. The claim to such a solution could then look like this:

Claim #: 'A piston 1 inside a volume of space 2, as illustrated in Fig. 1, both shaped in such a way that the piston 1, guided along the in-

ternal walls of the volume of space 2, is pressed by a spring 3 in such a way that it is held against a valve 4 located at one end of the volume of space 2."

Of course, this composition is not written in stone. Any number of ways of writing it is conceivable as long as the result is a strong claim. Another way would be to simply add another claim stating that a cylindrical volume is only an example and any shape of volume would suffice that allows the function of the piston according to the first claim.

The point here though is how easy it is to inadvertently introduce a hidden weakness by using seemingly innocuous terminology and how essential it is to keep a critical eye on what is being written. Other terms to watch out for are "spherical", "cube", "triangular", "square", "shaft" etc.

Caution with details in drawings.

Illustrations do not just support the description of the innovation; they also have the same legally binding relevance. Therefore, all illustrative details have the potential to offer weaknesses. For instance, depictions of nuts and bolts, welding beads, shapes of openings, references to machined surfaces, dimensions, references to stock materials etc.

Often technical drawings meant for the manufacture of prototypes or models are used as illustrations in patent specifications. Such drawings though contain far more information than is necessary or advisable for illustrations in a patent specification. It is therefore essential to purge all unnecessary details from a production drawing when used in a patent specification.

Cross-referencing similar or related patents

If the previous patent survey has found a patent or patents that come near to or are similar to the innovation at hand, the patent office might also find the same patents. Patent offices have a lot to do, they have no time to compare and weigh up patent claims, and will in such cases offhandedly declare prior art and refuse patent registration. That then costs time, money and nerves to disprove these allegations. This can be avoided by adding cross-references in the specification to these other patents. In these cross-references the innovation at hand is distinguished from the other patents and improvements or differences explained. Such cross-references will also make the patent protection stronger.

Another case for cross-referencing earlier patents is when an innovation builds on or integrates these and needs to be explained. These are called related patents or applications. Cross-referencing these would also arguably have the added benefit of saving lengthy descriptions as these would already be in the related patents. It is enough to give the title and registration number of cross-referenced patents.

Cross-referencing details within a patent specification

Ambiguity is the adversary of any legal document and this is particularly true of patent specifications. A strong patent avoids ambiguity by supporting cross-references to details.

To do this, all drawings, claims and component parts described or mentioned in a patent specification must be assigned a label and a reference number. Similar to technical production drawings, all drawings are labelled "Figure" or "Fig." followed by their reference number. The views and cross-sections in drawings are labelled "View" or "Cross-Section" followed by a reference number. Illustrated components are assigned just a number (without a label) in the drawings. These are then given a label only in the description and claims section such as "piston 1" or "valve 2". To avoid possible confusion with other reference numbers, these can also be written as "301" or "401" (all reference examples without inverted commas).

These reference numbers together with their labels can be used where needed in any text to clearly refer to the corresponding components in the drawings. The reference number of a component always immediately follows the mention of its designation. For instance:

"A piston 1 inside a volume of space 2, as illustrated in Fig. 1, both shaped in such a way that the piston 1, guided along the internal walls of the volume of space 2, is pressed by a spring 3 in such a way that it is held against a valve 4 allocated at one end of the volume of space 2."

When cross-referencing a claim, component or drawing from another patent the title and registration number of said patent precedes the references to the claim, component or drawing in that patent.

Filling In the Formalities

An explanation of the following patent sections according to USPTO guidelines:

(1) *Title of the Invention:*

Pretty obvious, but keep it short. Also, no "invented" or fantasy product names.

(2) *Cross-reference to related applications, (if any), Related applications may also be listed on an application data sheet, either instead of or together with being listed in the specification.)*

Again, pretty clear, this is where the names of any cross-referenced patents are placed.

(3) *Statement of federally sponsored research or development (if any)*

The dream of every independent inventor. This is where you indicate any sponsoring by the US government.

(4) *The names of the parties to a joint research agreement if the claimed invention was made as a result of activities within the scope of a joint research agreement.*

A lot of inventions are the results of group efforts. This is where they are all given a mention.

(5) *Reference to a "Sequence Listing," a table, or a computer program listing appendix submitted on a compact disc and an incor-*

poration by reference of the material on the compact disc. The total number of compact disc including duplicates and the files on each compact disc shall be specified.

This is where software engineers refer to the media on which their software innovations are stored.

(6) *Background of the Invention:*

Basically, this is where the current technology is described and the problem explained that the innovation at hand solves together with a statement that a ways and means of doing this is disclosed in the description section (9).

(7) *Brief Summary of the Invention*

This is meant to be the short version of section (9) usually without cross-references and claims. Because everything in this section is not legally binding; that is, does not contribute to the patent's protection properties; the description here is composed more for easy reading rather than crafted and convoluted to avoid weaknesses and loopholes. If there are drawings, one of them, usually the one offering the most information should be included here.

(8) *Brief description of the several views of the drawing (if any)*

Here all the illustrations and any other views, cross-sections etc. are listed with their reference numbers and a short description of what they illustrate.

(9) *Detailed Description of the Invention*

This is the all-important disclosure of the innovation. Whatever is written in this section is legally binding and forms the basis of what the patent is protecting.

(10) *A claim or claims*

Here the claims made in section (9) are numbered and listed separately. Like in section (9), anything written here is legally binding and forms part of the patent protection.

(11) *Abstract of the disclosure*

This is an even shorter summary of what is in section (7) and is supposed to be no longer than 150 words (according to US guidelines).

Most patent offices distinguish between the inventor, the applicant of the patent and who ultimately owns the patent rights. These are entered into the application form when filing for patent registration and are later displayed in the heading of the patent specification document. In the case of independent inventors, all three will be the same person. This can change though if the patent is sold and the new ownership is registered at the patent office. Then the name of the owner is accordingly revised, but the name of the inventor always remains.

Some last advice to this chapter

Before starting to draw up a specification, it is well worth the time to first read through a few professionally written ones to get the "feel" of how they are written, how they are composed and how the authors express themselves. It is important to note how the documents are formatted, which of course is best done using a word processor with a wide choice of formatting tools. It is not a rush job done on the move, it takes time, patience and due diligence. Professionals usually take six to eight weeks; a novice should reckon with at least twice as long. A lot of thought has to be put into the work, making a first draft, reflecting on it, improving and amending it, even sleeping over it. It is also worth it to sometimes just take a break for a day or two and gain some distance before carrying on.

And last but not least, in all honesty a novice's document probably will not be as polished as that of a patent lawyer. But that's okay and anyway not the point. Just like an average car driver showing his skills on a race course cannot take the curves as expertly as a professional racing driver, his aim is to arrive safely at the finishing line, the aim here is to end up with a patent that sufficiently protects intellectual property, even if it takes twice as long and does not have quite that professional touch to it.

Applying For Patent Registration

The patent specification has finally been drawn up and is ready for patent registration. The address for this will be found on the website of the local national patent office. Most patent offices offer two options for this, a "nonprovisional" and a "provisional" registration. The USPTO even offers three options, a nonprovisional for large entities, such as large companies, a provisional reserved for small entities such as small start-ups, and a second type of provisional for micro entities such as independent inventors. Apart from a discount on the registration fee, provisional applications also have slightly laxer requirements than the full blown nonprovisional version. Among other things the patent office does not research the merit of the patent (do a survey for prior art), which also costs a considerable fee, and the duration of the provisional registration is not counted to the twenty-year duration of the final patent (according to US law).

Note: In the US it is important to clearly specify that a provisional application is requested in the case of an independent inventor or a micro entity to secure a discount. In some countries, Germany and Austria for instance, the provisional registration is the norm even for large entities before later filing for a nonprovisional registration.

Note: there is a caveat to provisional applications; they have a time limit, usually 12 months, after which a nonprovisional application must be made. Failing to do so will automatically invalidate the patent. It is a good idea to find out at the local national patent office what the time limit is, some even offer 18 months.

Most patent offices will send a reminder before the deadline is past, but it is inadvisable to rely too heavily on this.

The fee for a nonprovisional registration (in digital form) in the US is 300 US dollars plus 660 US dollars for the mandatory patent survey. The fee for a small entity using the provisional option is 150 US dollars and 75 US dollars for a micro entity. Fees in other countries can vary heavily from these. In Germany for instance a provisional registration filed on paper costs 60 euros and 40 euros if filed electronically (all fees mentioned are from 2016).

Regardless what option is chosen, after filing an application the patent office first checks the specification document for irregularities. If they find anything, they will request it amended accordingly. Otherwise, after a few days a certificate of registration with the registration number, patent title, name of owner, applicant and inventor, the date, and in some countries even time of day, will arrive. This document serves as proof of ownership of the patent rights and represents an object of value in its own right.

Capitalising On Your Innovation

With this document in hand, the inventor is now free to capitalise on his or her idea. There are basically two ways of doing this. One way would be to start a business on the basis of the innovation using the patent to solicit financial backing, maybe through a crowd funding scheme, what is called a start-up in today's parlance. This implies having the nerves, energy and knowhow to start such a venture from scratch and is far beyond the scope of this book.

Finding Prospective Industry Partners

Most independent inventors plan on approaching prospective industry partners, usually manufacturers of goods, in the hope they will be interested. In this case it is worth noting just how important it is to approach the right persons. Only very few people have the capacity to appreciate the potential of an innovation, especially if confronted with just a few drawings. Sales reps for instance will at best just shrug their shoulders and wish the inventor well. The people with the highest likelihood of showing interest and also have the influence to bring a new product to market are the heads of R&D, CEOs, and maybe marketing chiefs. These are the people whose attention one needs to attract.

There are a number of ways of doing this, some more effective than others. One is to do the rounds at exhibitions and trade fairs or even become an exhibitor. Some trade fairs offer stands for small businesses and inventors at reduced fees, but usually in out-of-the-way halls that companies tend to spurn. This costs time that an independent inventor does not really have - remember, the provisional application runs out after twelve months. It is also expensive having to pay stall fees and staying the nights somewhere in a different city, all on the off-chance that just the right person finds his way to the stall.

A more direct approach is generally more effective, that is, contacting potentially interested companies. But just turning up on the doorstep is a bad idea. People who run companies have tight schedules and are not willing to fit some random person into that who just appeared in their secretary's office. Phoning up is not much different, it is the secretary's job to keep phone calls to their boss down to a minimum. Someone on the phone claiming to have the best idea since the invention of the transistor will not make much difference. And anyway, in the end most likely the person most qualified to judge any kind of innovation will not be available at that particular moment. Emails are also not a good idea. There is a danger of these landing in a spam directory or offhandedly sorted out by the secretary trying to mitigate the deluge of mails to his/her boss.

Contact per "snail mail", even in this day and age of internet and instant messaging, offers the most promise of success. A brown A4 envelope or equivalent containing an introductory letter mentioning the patent - note: under no circumstances indicate that it is a DIY patent - a general description of the idea and its advantages (but not the convoluted description in the patent specification. It is important to keep it concise and easy to understand), drawings and maybe a few photos should impress a likely secretary enough to forward it to the boss instead of throwing it in the waste. Also important is to address the letter to the correct person within the company, see above. Most companies have websites where this information is to be found. If one has an academic degree or title, regardless what, do not be too modest to use it in the return address. All this information must be sent to all potentially interested parties within a single day.

What happens next will be a good indicator of just how high a market potential the innovation really has. A fairly high potential should result in most recipients reaching out, usually by phone, within a week or two. These might include invitations to come around to personally present the idea. Any working models should be taken to such meetings. Others might instead ask for production drawings or comprehensive sketches so that they can try out the innovation themselves in their own workshops. Or they might suggest sending someone around. Whatever happens, it is important to be well prepared.

Negotiating a Contract

If all goes well, the inventor will eventually find him-/herself sitting at a table across from CEOs or their executives, the more the better, negotiating possible agreements. Most of these will probably be unwilling to settle for less than straight out buying the patent or, failing that, insist on an exclusive licence. It is important to understand the pros and cons of these two choices. With an exclusive licencing arrangement, the patent remains in the inventor's ownership together with all the obligations of upholding the patent. That is, the responsibility to apply for the inevitable nonprovisional registration, to pay the yearly patent fees, to carry the costs of foreign patent registrations if any, to pursue patent rights infringements and to fight off possible challenges. Most of that is well beyond the abilities of an inventor and would require the services of a patent lawyer together will the costs this instigates. Ceding ownership of the patent frees the inventor of these obligations, but there are risks involved in this depending on what model of commission is chosen. More on this a little later.

Whichever way is decided, the next question will be the form of commission. There are two main models, a one-off commission or regular payment in royalties. Financially, a one-off commission is generally not advantageous for the inventor. This is because it is almost impossible to gauge the true value of an untested innovation and predict its future success. Companies will therefore tend to make offers far below the perceived potential value of an innovation. To an inventor accustomed to working within very limited means, typically far out classed by experienced company executives and usually even less knowledgeable of the true value of their innovation, this offer might appear quite generous and fair - it nearly never is - and accept it. The only real advantage of a one-off commission is that the inventor can then wash their hands of any future costs and risks.

The second approach, payment in royalties, which is just another word for a cut of the wholesale price per unit, looks more promising. It secures a fair share in the future success of the innovation and can add up over the years to quite a large sum of money. But this comprises risks if combined with ceding ownership of the patent. For instance, the manufacturer might for some reason change his mind about marketing the new product and shelf the patent leaving the inventor high and dry. He might decide to offer licences to third parties without feeling obliged to share the proceeds with the inventor. Or what happens if the manufacturer goes bankrupt? In this scenario a receiver could decide to sell off the company assets including the patent. There is nothing saying the new owner will feel obliged to honour the contract with the former owner. In such an event bad blood and expensive time-consuming court cases could be the outcome.

This is not to say that manufacturers are generally devious rogues. Quite the opposite, in almost all cases they are honest negotiators genuinely interested in reaching an agreement mutually beneficial to both sides. But no one can say what the future holds.

There are a few ways to help mitigate these risks; one of them is to take a good look at who the negotiating partner is. Are they a small young setup, maybe working on a shoe string and a lot of enthusiasm? Or are they a much larger, older business with a portfolio of successful products? The latter will almost surely be the less risky partner. Openly addressing the above issues will show if the other side can be taken seriously. A serious negotiation partner will not try to shrug such reservations off and will more likely offer a few solutions.

In return, the inventor should also offer solutions. For instance, a joint ownership of the patent. This would protect the inventor's interests in case of a bankruptcy (it is important here to be clear who is responsible for upholding the patent) and give them a say over licences to third parties. A full return of ownership of the patent could be agreed on if the planned product is not marketed within a certain time limit, i.e., twelve months from date of signing the contract. These are all just suggestions and maybe other solutions are better applicable, but being openly prepared to tackle these issues is the mark of a serious negotiator who knows what he wants.

If a royalties-based commission is agreed on, the next step is to decide if this is a fixed sum per unit or a percentage of the price of each unit. A fixed sum is more practical if the innovation is a component of a far larger complex product, such as an engine or machine and does not change the overall characteristics of this product. The disadvantage here though is that the royalties will steadily depreciate with inflation over the twenty-year course of the patent. This can be mitigated by agreeing to have royalties reviewed and adjusted every year.

If the innovation embodies the whole product or improves an existing one so inherently that it can be considered a new type of product, then percentage-based royalties serve an inventor's interests better. For practical reasons this is generally calculated as a percentage of the wholesale price usually without the cost of packaging.

Caution is advised if the product is manufactured in a different country and imported! Many companies have their goods manufactured abroad at low cost and practice huge price mark-ups after they arrive at their inland warehouses. In such cases it should be made clear that royalties are based on the wholesale price the company charges inland retailers and not the one the company pays the foreign factory.

How high royalties are depends on negotiating skills, the market potential of the innovation, the number of units sold per year and the price per unit.

Two examples: a tin can manufacturer delivers around a billion units a year at an average wholesale price of five US dollar cents per unit. Already 0.2% royalties per unit would add up to one hundred thousand US dollars of royalties per year. On the other hand, a large bicycle helmet manufacturer might deliver fifty thousand units per year at an average wholesale price of thirty US dollars. Here to reach the same amount of royalties per year as in the example of the tin can manufacturer one would have to ask for almost seven per cent royalties on each unit. For a consumer product this is quite high and would depend heavily on how good the innovation is to be achievable.

It is therefore not too bold to ask a negotiation partner for projected production volumes and wholesale prices before negotiating royalties. Also, it is good negotiation practice to begin at high prices and see what the other side says. One can always go down, but it is not so easy to go up again.

If all goes well, ultimately a contract is drawn up. Usually this is done by the company's lawyer, which is all fine and good but under no circumstances should it be blindly signed. It should rather be considered as a draft for one's own lawyer to read through and if necessary, suggest a few amendments. The other side might do the same with these revisions until both sides finally come to agree on one contract version.

A Few Last Words

It is in the nature of the subject that even when following the best advice failure can still never be ruled out. Should this happen, it might be of consolation to know that some of the most accomplished inventors had to try four or five times before finally achieving success. Remember, only successes are celebrated; failures are never reported. This book was written with just that in mind, to put the independent inventor in a position to be able to try and try again until they finally succeed.

Michael Kobzan

About The Author

Michael Kobzan lives in Berlin, Germany with his wife. He is a self-employed design engineer, industrial designer, design consultant and has also worked as a guest professor in the field of 3D-art and computer aided industrial design at the University of Applied Science in Potsdam, German. Apart from numerous novels, he is also the author of a number of books on the subject of 3D-art, computer visualisation and in the field of intellectual property rights.

Other Books by This Author

John Dunley

John Dunley is a former elite space marine in the New Caledonian armed forces. Court-martialled on false charges, stripped of all his honours and imprisoned, he escapes and works as an independent spacer specialised in semi-legal work for mostly unsavoury clients. Just two things drive him, finding his deported family and revenge for the false charges against him. His luck seems to turn when he is offered a contract to rescue New Caledonia's crown prince who has crash-landed on a planet inside rebel territory in return for information that will lead to the return of his family. There is just one problem, the client is the man responsible for the false charges against him.

Unvirtual

A company specialised in 3D computer games develops the ultimate gaming computer. It generates virtual reality environments indistinguishable from physical reality. An unscrupulous billionaire with the support of rogue government elements plans to use this new technology to solve the unemployment problems of a stubborn global recession. It will cost the lives of 95% of the global population if he succeeds.

Unknown Enemy

The envoy of an advanced alien civilisation lands his ship on present day earth and offers advanced technology in return for earth's alliance in a 400-year-old war against an aggressive alien species. Within a few decades earth develops into an interstellar civilisation and sends its first interstellar ship, the Nelson, on its first combat mission. The ship returns to earth after its mission to find that 150 years on earth have gone by and is led by a corrupt president and his family with the support of an unscrupulous oligarchy.

Khufu

Dr Harriet Henning, a young archaeologist, stumbles across clay steles marked with strange unknown cuneiforms inside an ancient Egyptian tomb. She manages to photograph them before the tomb collapses and buries everything. Within days of her discovery, dark forces begin to harass and threaten her for the photographs. Wondering what can be so important about these tablets, she decides to team up with a friend and her uncle to decipher the cuneiforms for themselves. These turn out to uncover a 4500-year-old secret.

Don't miss out!

Visit the website below and you can sign up to receive emails whenever Mike Kobzan publishes a new book. There's no charge and no obligation.

https://books2read.com/r/B-A-HDQKC-AYYYE

BOOKS 2 READ

Connecting independent readers to independent writers.

Also by Mike Kobzan

Khufu
Unvirtual
The Inventor's Guide to Success

Watch for more at www.formwandel.com.

About the Author

UK ex-patriot living and working in Berlin, Germany as a freelance Industrial designer, engineer and writer. Married, two children. Special interests are long distant cycling and motorcycle tours through Europe and writing about my experiences.

Read more at www.formwandel.com.

www.ingramcontent.com/pod-product-compliance
Lightning Source LLC
Chambersburg PA
CBHW061358140726
47997CB00003B/1258